Sacagawea's Son

BY ALBERT FURTWANGLER

OHS neg. OrHi 17459

Oregon Historical Society Press
Portland

◌

A reprint from the *Oregon Historical Quarterly*
THE JOURNAL OF RECORD FOR OREGON HISTORY

Cover image: This model of Sacagawea with her son on her back served as the basis for their depiction in the *Corps of Discovery* statue that overlooks the Missouri River at Clark's Point in Kansas City, Missouri. Experts on Shoshone and Hidatsa culture and physiology worked with the sculptor, Eugene Daub, to ensure authenticity in the physical details, clothing, and basketry. The completed sculpture includes Lewis, Clark, York (Clark's black slave), and Lewis's Newfoundland dog, Seaman, on their return voyage from the Pacific in the fall of 1806. Used courtesy of Eugene Daub, sculptor and photographer, 2000.

Revised and reprinted from *Oregon Historical Quarterly*
Fall 2001, Volume 102, Number 3 and Winter 2001, Volume 102, Number 4
by the Oregon Historical Society Press
1200 S.W. Park Ave., Portland, OR 97205-2483
www.ohs.org
press@ohs.org

Printed in the United States of America
Printed on acid-free paper ∞

The *Oregon Historical Quarterly* is published quarterly — Spring, Summer, Fall, and Winter — by the Oregon Historical Society and is a benefit of membership in the Society. For information about membership, contact the Membership Office, Oregon Historical Society, 1200 S.W. Park Avenue, Portland, OR 97205-2483; (503) 222-1741; orhist@ohs.org. For subscriptions and single issues, write press@ohs.org.

Sacagawea's Son

～

Jean Baptiste Charbonneau as a Symbol

BY ALBERT FURTWANGLER

IN 2000, SACAGAWEA'S child came out of the footnotes of history to an enduring fame around the world. His image — or the image of a baby representing him — now shines on a brightly minted dollar coin, and his story is sure to be publicized and retold often through the bicentennial celebrations of the Lewis and Clark expedition of 1803–1806. In Oregon, a rededication took place on June 24, 2000, at his grave site near Jordan Valley in the southeast corner of the state. It was an occasion for clearing and improving the site as a tourist attraction and for highlighting Oregon's claim to an important person in the expedition. The grave site has long been a pilgrimage destination for Lewis and Clark devotees. It has been on the National Register of Historic Places since 1971, after the site was developed and dedicated through the efforts of local people and Oregon members of the Lewis and Clark Trail Heritage Foundation.

But what can we say about the person whose life ended in Oregon in 1866? The signboard at the site outlines a tantalizing history. The child was born on February 11, 1805, at the winter camp of Lewis and Clark on the Upper Missouri (in what is now North Dakota). Just a few weeks later the party headed west and the child came along, survived risks and hardships over thousands of miles, and returned safely in 1806. Just days after Meriwether Lewis and William Clark parted downriver, Clark sent a letter back to the boy's father, Toussaint Charbonneau, making an offer to educate the child and treat him as his own. After an interval, the child (by now named Jean Baptiste Charbonneau and nicknamed Pomp) was brought to St. Louis and educated at Clark's expense. A further turn of fortune lay ahead. In 1822, a European prince, Paul Wilhelm of Württemberg, ascended the Missouri on an expedition of scientific curiosity. He met the youth, still in his teens, near the mouth of the Kansas River and agreed to carry him along to Europe on his return. From 1824 to 1829, the young man lived at a palace in Germany and may have traveled elsewhere in Europe. When he returned, he once more looked to the West. He was a mountain man, guide, interpreter, and adventurer over routes leading from St. Louis to California, where he took part in gold mining after 1849. He was on a further adventure to search for gold in Montana when he became ill near the Owyhee River and died in May 1866.

These bare facts can be documented and fleshed out a little, but not really very much.[1] Despite eager searches, the life records that have emerged consist almost entirely of passing references in other people's journals. This is an odd turn of events. A life of sixty-one years, touching many lands, led by an educated man who was surely fluent in several languages, now endures in just a few lines and images built up from a handful of odd passages and details; and all our impressions of this life have been composed by others.

Because this life story is now a matter of concentrated interest, it lies prey to further distortion through modern publicity. In a word, Sacagawea's child has long been a symbolic figure, a person whose life story points a moral or whose image serves mainly to focus feelings or attitudes about other subjects or ideas — such as Sacagawea as a mother, the character of William Clark, or the exploration and settlement of the West. We would do well to ask pointedly what kind of symbol he has become, or is becoming, and how the available evidence supports such developments.

THE CEREMONIES at the grave site in 2000 are a good instance of the problem at hand. In the course of an hour or two, several distinct groups laid claim to Jean Baptiste Charbonneau and included him in their particular symbol systems. At the opening, the local parish priest blessed and sprinkled water on the grave of Charbonneau, who had been named for a Christian saint and properly baptized as a Catholic in 1809. At the close, several representatives of Native American tribes joined in a circle around the grave and conducted rituals that were too sacred to be photographed or recorded — thus claiming the child Pomp or Pompy as their kinsman and spiritual brother. Local scout troops raised a fifteen-star flag on a high pole at the site to claim an early American and a young person like themselves. They led a pledge of allegiance. Members of different Lewis and Clark organizations made remarks about the child of the expedition. A local rancher and organizer traced the history of the site and the family history around it. The audience was made up largely of local people, appreciating the site as a link between their small community and the wider history of America and the West. Many took part in a lively re-enactment before the ceremonies with a stagecoach drawn by a six-horse team and accompanied by a small troop of uniformed cavalry. The final note in the air was taps, played by a bugler in uniform on horseback — doing military honors for Charbonneau as the heir of Captains Lewis and Clark and their soldiers and as the guide (in the 1840s) of the Mormon Battalion.

It may seem wholesome that a single figure could unite such disparate interests in one common place and event. Many participants referred to that

Statue in Washington Park, Portland, Oregon, of Sacagawea carrying her infant son

notion, in fact. The ceremony was an occasion for American or western good feeling, with a feast afterward at the public park in Jordan Valley, to which all were invited. Obviously, however, such a high point of reconciliation implies a history of strife. Cavalry and Indians, Christians and spirit healers, Shoshones and Mandans, ranchers and miners, and the peoples they displaced have not been such boon companions over the past two centuries. Can one man's life story serve to relax all these tensions? In fact, the participants in the ceremony sometimes showed a justified nervousness even in saying his name. Was it properly Baptiste? Jean-Baptiste? J.B.? Charbonneau? Pomp? Pompey? Son of Sacajawea? Or should that be Sacagawea? Each variation still can be taken amiss, as a symbol of alliances one way and exclusions another.

Fortunately, there is helpful suggestion for such perplexities in the journals of Meriwether Lewis. On February 11, 1805, Lewis wrote: "about five oclock this evening one of the wives of Charbono was delivered of a fine boy."[2] The alert explorer then went on to note further details of the birth, including a tension or conflict about its significance:

it is worthy of remark that this was the first child which this woman had boarn and as is common in such cases her labour was tedious and the pain violent; Mr. Jessome [a trader at the Mandan villages, used by Lewis as an interpreter] informed me that he had frequently administered a small portion of the rattle of the rattle-snake, which he assured me had never failed to produce the desired effect, that of hastening the birth of the child; having the rattle of a snake by me I gave it to him and he administered two rings of it to the woman broken in small pieces with the fingers and added to a small quantity of water.

Just in these lines we can see several strains of belief and doubt about different cultures and their practices. Lewis, the English-speaking scientific observer, carefully records the circumstances of the woman's hard labor and the strange remedy proposed by a French-speaking intermediary to the Indians. He records the exact dose. Yet, it is a pinch, made by fingers, of a raw animal substance, an American home remedy, almost certainly something learned from Indian midwives. Lewis's words seem to catch a hesitation in midair: René Jusseaume's need to emphatically "assure me" that this odd remedy "never failed to produce the desired effect." Thus assured, Lewis actually complies and reaches for the ingredient at hand. Thus armed, Jusseaume confidently administers his potion. Thus doctored, the mother promptly gives birth. That hard, final fact is what makes the whole incident "worthy of remark."

Lewis goes on to provide a further general reflection:

Whether this medicine was truly the cause or not I shall not undertake to determine, but I was informed that she had not taken it more than ten minutes before she brought

Grave of Jean Baptiste Charbonneau near Jordan Valley, Oregon

forth perhaps the remedy may be worthy of future experiments, but I must confess I want faith as to it's efficacy.[3]

Lewis not only doubts but he also allows that there are reasons to doubt his own doubting. Readers familiar with his journals will recognize a typical thoughtful evenness here in his presentation of something new and extraordinary. He presents a generous account of what he has directly observed, acknowledges his own puzzlement, and leaves room for "future experiments" or wider investigations.[4]

Lewis's example offers us a strong admonition. In years to come we are sure to see this child of the wondrous birth as a symbol of many fine ideals, including human equality, peaceful intentions, and benevolent nurture. He can easily be thought of as a typical figure from a particular era in America and the West. His life connects east and west, old Europe and new California, in some fascinating dynamics of refined learning and raw experience. A wise reader or interpreter, however, must proceed with Lewis-like circumspection. Every such development of this symbolic figure can be grounded in solid information and persuasive assurances as strong as Jusseaume's about his snake medicine. That information also reveals a darker side at every turn

— a touch of venom, as it were, from the other end of the snake. The memorable incidents and images of Sacagawea's son are matters to ponder rather than to blindly celebrate.

The most obvious and widespread symbol, of course, is the babe on the new dollar coin. He has reached such worldwide celebrity by dint of very modern political pressures — riding both literally and figuratively on his mother's back. Congress was pressed to issue dollar coins and had to endorse a widely appealing female figure for its design. The Susan B. Anthony dollar coin of 1979 failed to gain wide acceptance, and great wrangles would have ensued if a more popular coin emerged, displacing that feminist icon with anything but another great woman. The final vote for Sacagawea was almost unanimous — in favor of a female figure who is at once famous, young, heroic, legendary, timely, and indigenous.

Sacagawea and Jean Baptiste on the dollar coin

There have been complaints that such a choice was all too pat and made worse in a "kitschy" design by a trendy female sculptor, but there are easy rejoinders to such criticism.[5] This is a new coin for a new century, intended to revitalize old habits with American currency. The ancient caution applies to any coin with a human face: "Render unto Caesar the things which are Caesar's." The image and superscription stamp the coin with a mark of ownership; to pay taxes is to render back to the central government the coin that it has minted. Like the ancient emperors, the American figures of Washington, Jefferson, Lincoln, and even Franklin Roosevelt and John Kennedy appear on our coins in formal profiles. They circulate as our sculpted demigods. The new coin is impudent toward such imagery, though not really subversive of it. It strikes a different pose. Here at last is a founding mother to face the Founding Fathers, a fresh young person to rival the seasoned presidents, an Indian with a name and particular story to supplant the stoical Indian of the old nickel, a golden person of color on our basic measure of value. If the design seems informal or even vulgar, it thereby suits the promise of democracy, that value derives from the common people, not aristocrats. Even a sleeping baby has a rightful place on our coin: all are created equal.

But as a symbol of equality, this new coin bears a deeper blemish if we look at it honestly. Its faces are the faces of children, who in fact were held and forced along in rough subordination in 1805. At the time of her baby's birth, Sacagawea was still a girl in her early teens. She was not properly Charbonneau's wife but one of several Indian women he possessed over a long lifetime; he had two or three such women when he met Lewis and Clark. Worse yet, Sacagawea was a Shoshone child, captured by Hidatsa raiders when she was eleven or twelve, carried hundreds of miles away, and traded. Nicholas Biddle, who prepared the first full narrative of the expedition, states that "she was sold as a slave to Chaboneau, who brought her up and afterward married her."[6] Many a statue has Sacagawea pointing the way west as a noble guide to Lewis and Clark — and, in fact, she did recognize some landmarks very helpfully — but she was hardly a volunteer. Her travels west and back were forced upon her soon after childbirth. She was famously brought back to a reunion with her own people but then carried onward again as a matter of course. Her baby was thrust along with her into months of risk, illness, malnutrition, and isolation in a company of rough, male adventurers. She lived perforce among aliens who spoke another language. Charbonneau might well have said what Humbert Humbert says so tellingly of Lolita during another long tour of America. Every night they "made it up very gently. You see, she had absolutely nowhere else to go."[7]

THE SIGNBOARD AT THE GRAVE site states that "Baptiste and his mother symbolized the peaceful nature of the 'Corps of Discovery.'" This is a symbolism directly documented by the explorers' journals, of course, and repeated in many well-known paintings. A conspicuous mother and child showed that approaching canoes did not carry a war party. On October 19, 1805, Clark recorded this point in a dramatic incident. That day he entered several mat lodges along the riverside on the Columbia Plateau. Indians had fled into them as he approached and sat inside in great agitation, "some crying and ringing there [sic] hands, others hanging their heads."[8] Clark had shot off a gun nearby and now every effort to show a friendly disposition failed him. He held out his hand, offered presents, and smoked with the men, but without much success. Then Lewis arrived by canoe, and the mood changed instantly:

as Soon as they Saw the Squar wife of the interperters they pointed to her and informed those who continued yet in the Same position I first found them, they imediately all came out and appeared to assume new life, the sight of This Indian woman, wife to one

This model of Sacagawea served as the basis for her depiction in the Corps of Discovery statue that overlooks the Missouri River at Clark's Point in Kansas City, Missouri. Experts on Shoshone and Hidatsa culture and physiology worked with the sculptor, Eugene Daub, to ensure authenticity in her physical details, clothing, and basketry. The completed sculpture includes Lewis, Clark, York (Clark's black slave), and Lewis's Newfoundland dog, Seaman, on their return voyage from the Pacific in the fall of 1806.

of our interprs. confirmed those people of our friendly intentions, as no woman ever accompanies a war party of Indians in this quarter —.[9]

A similar entry appears on a rough sketch map of the Columbia River from this period: "The wife of Shabono our interpetr we find reconsiles all the Indians, as to our friendly intentions a woman with a party of men is a token of peace."[10]

To be perceived as a woman, of course, Sacagawea would have to be seen as a member of the party, visible from afar, and conspicuously female. Thereby hangs a problem. The simplest way to make her stand out would be to set her apart, elevate her a bit, and make sure she was holding or carrying her baby. That would also set her and her child up as preeminently vulnerable. They would have been prime targets if a newly encountered village were to prove hostile, unfamiliar with this Upper Columbia symbolism, or wildly agitated by a party such as Clark's that came bristling with guns and shooting them off at passing wildlife.

Charles M. Russell's *Lewis and Clark on the Lower Columbia* is a widely known image of Sacagawea and her son in such an ambiguous situation. The painting has circulated in thousands of copies as the cover illustration on two popular and authoritative books.[11] It shows three large canoes bearing down on a smaller vessel in which Sacagawea stands upright, her baby strapped to her back, holding her arms forward to make signal gestures with her hands. Russell's painting, of course, is an imaginative creation, but it is likely an image remembered or half-remembered by many readers who think that "Baptiste and his mother symbolized the peaceful nature of the 'Corps of Discovery.'" A close look shows that the approaching Indian canoes have no visible weapons; every hand on board seems to be holding an oar. Sacagawea's boat has two gun barrels poking out over the gunwales, and Captain Clark stands alert at the prow with a long-barreled gun in the crook of his arm. If this depiction is at all like any incident of first encounter, we might well ask just who is at greatest risk of getting hurt.

Even if mother and child were symbols of peace at first encounter, how innocently can we claim long-range peaceful intentions? The journals report many encounters where Lewis and Clark proclaimed peace, awarded symbolic peace medals, and exhorted new peacemaking between enemy tribes. James Ronda's solid study of these efforts, however, discloses many failures and misunderstandings. He concludes that the captains developed remarkable friendly relations when they were face-to-face with many western peoples, but they were naive on the level of large-scale diplomacy. "The explorers comprehended neither river economics nor plains politics," Ronda writes. "In a world where 'peace' meant 'truce' and where warriors fought one day and traded the next, Lewis and Clark were simply unable and sometimes unwilling to face the facts of native life."[12]

Inescapably, they came west leading a heavily armed military force for purposes of empire. They were specifically directed to press across the continent and lay claim to new territory. They were instructed to avoid conflict, but Jefferson was clearly determined to have them and their successors explore and develop American trade routes from coast to coast. The Spanish authorities understood such invasion as a threat. The Teton Sioux saw it as a manifest challenge to their power. One band of Piegan Blackfeet was alarmed enough to engage in a gunfight with Lewis.

The issues of clashing empires may seem far afield from the symbolism of an infant on his mother's back, but in the end we do have to ask: Were these young figures actually used as pawns in a gambit of great peril? Would anyone now put a teenage girl and her baby on the front lines of a global conflict? Could the "peaceful nature" of the Corps have allowed pushing white children forward that way? Perhaps Lewis and Clark were wiser on this point than later writers and artists. When Lewis set out to seek a first encounter with Shoshones near the Continental Divide, he might well have taken Sacagawea along as the one person in the party who spoke the Shoshone language. When he made up an advance party on August 9, 1805, however, he took three trusted men, including his best hunter, and left Sacagawea and her child to follow with Clark's larger, safer group.

THE MOTHER AND CHILD ON THE NEW coin are symbols of equality; in some first encounters on the expedition, they served as symbols of peace. In both cases, as we have seen, the imagery is largely an effect of contrast. On the coin, fresh figures stand out, quite unlike the staid, sculpted heads of national leaders. In the canoe, these young figures appear soft and vulnerable, unlike their rough-and-ready armed escorts. Underlying these symbolisms, however, there is an intrinsic image, one that directly appeals to our feelings. Mother and child make a familiar symbol of intimate, affectionate nurture. In this aspect, Sacagawea appears as a madonna of the wilderness. We often see her represented as a brave, protective, caring, somewhat older woman, and she draws our tender feelings toward herself in sympathy to what we assume were her own devoted feelings toward her child. Moreover, she and the child impart a softer touch to the entire Corps of Discovery. They appear as a precious cargo at the center of the tableau. In records necessarily crammed with hard, dry facts, they emerge from time to time in incidents of drama and human appeal. The child in particular becomes an object of concern and affection, who leaves a pang in the heart when the explorers must part from him at last.

Again, the expedition records yield solid evidence to support this nurture symbolism and to justify further elaborations. But the records also force us to temper our feelings, if we read them with full attention. The

Charbonneau family did have a special and privileged place in the expedition, for it rode in the captains' vessel and slept in the captains' quarters. The journals are quite explicit. On the day of departure from Fort Mandan, Lewis noted: "Capt. Clark myself the two Interpretters and the woman and child sleep in a tent of dressed skins." A few days later, he wrote that the white pirogue was considered the safest vessel and accordingly carried "our instruments, Papers, medicine and the most valuable part of the merchandize which we had still in reserve as presents for the Indians. we had also embarked on board ourselves, with three men . . . . and the squaw with the young child." Twice this vessel had dangerous accidents when a nervous Charbonneau was at the helm. When the pirogue nearly capsized on May 14, 1805, Lewis credited Sacagawea with rescuing invaluable items: "the Indian woman to whom I ascribe equal fortitude and resolution, with any person onboard at the time of the accedent, caught and preserved most of the light articles which were washed overboard."[13]

There were obvious practical reasons for keeping the Charbonneaus close at hand. Interpreters might be needed immediately in any surprise encounter. And perhaps the captains understood from the first that a woman and child would look good next to the leaders. Besides, the interpreters were civilians, and it would be inviting trouble to put the one woman in the party in close quarters with the enlisted men.

In any event, the infant in this group spent his first year close to the captains; and by journey's end, he had grown into the particular affections of William Clark. Very likely, Clark named Pompey's Pillar (or "Pompy's Tower," as Clark spelled it) — a landmark he sighted and climbed on the return trip, near present-day Billings, Montana — after his nickname for the child.[14] Clark thus attached the child's name to a place he also claimed as his own, for he carved his own name and the date into the rock. It remains there as the one intentional mark of the expedition that is still visible on the trail. Clark's fondness grew even deeper. When the time for parting came at the Mandan villages in August 1806, Clark wanted to carry the child along as his own.

"I offered to take his little Son," he wrote in the journals, "a butifull promising Child who is 19 months old." The parents put him off until the child had been weaned — perhaps in a year, if Clark were still willing — but Clark persisted.[15] Just a few days later, he sent Charbonneau a remarkable, confidential letter, opening several options by which the interpreter could make a better life for himself. He could be set up as a farmer; he could return to Montreal and explore options there; he could be outfitted to return west with Clark's backing as an interpreter or trader — just so long as Clark could watch over the boy. This pressure is repeated in line after line. "As to your little Son (my boy *Pomp*) you well know my fondness for him and my anxiety to take and raise him as my own child. I once more tell you if you will

Charbonneau continues to be a subject for artists, especially as the bicentennial of the Lewis and Clark expedition draws closer. Here, artist Roy Reynolds celebrates Charbonneau's life as a guide and mountain man.

bring your son Baptiest to me I will educate him and treat him as my own child." And again: "If you wish to return as an Interpreter . . . or if you wish to return to trade with the indians and will leave your little *Son Pomp* with me, I will assist you." And again: if Charbonneau is "desposed to accept either of my offers," then the boy should be brought and his mother "had best come along with you to take care of the boy untill I get him." Clark presses on with explicit instructions on how to reach him when the family gets to St. Louis, then closes with the same refrain: "with anxious expectations of seeing my little danceing boy Baptiest."[16]

This eager letter might seem an impulsive, momentary effusion, but Clark kept pressing until he fulfilled his plan. After many months, Charbonneau did bring the mother and child to St. Louis, and Clark kept his promises in return. The family must have arrived in St. Louis by 1809, for a baptismal record for the child, dated December 20 of that year, has recently been discovered there.[17] Clark helped Charbonneau acquire a tract of land near St. Louis in 1810, then bought it back in 1811 when Charbonneau changed his mind and headed back up the Missouri. The child remained in Clark's care, at least until 1820, for Clark's accounts show payments that year for tuition, board, lodging, and other expenses for J.B. Charbonneau.[18]

The full details of the arrangement are irrecoverable. We cannot say what Clark's motives were at first or what they came to be over time. Was he so infatuated with the child that even as a bachelor army officer with uncertain prospects he wanted to keep him near? Did he feel uneasy about his close companions of the expedition, once the reality of their parting was at hand? Clark's expedition journals note many Indian villages along the Missouri that had been decimated by disease. He may well have seen Charbonneau's move to St. Louis as a matter of life and death. His repeated appeals in his letter may well have that implied edge to them. As years passed, however, Clark became a different figure in the West. In 1807, he became superintendent of Indian affairs for Louisiana Territory and brigadier general of its militia. After Lewis's death in 1809, he succeeded him as territorial governor. Meanwhile, Clark had married the sixteen-year-old Julia Hancock in 1808 and established a permanent home in St. Louis, where he soon had children of his own. In 1813, Clark's name was inserted on a court document as the guardian of the infant children of Toussaint Charbonneau, when Charbonneau had disappeared and was presumed dead.[19] At that point, was Clark invoked as a caring personal friend or merely as the appropriate public figure?

Clark's account records refer to tuition, school supplies, and clothing payments made for the benefit of "Charbonneau, a half-Indian" or "a half-Indian boy." They also include payment for boarding, lodging, and washing. In other words, in 1820, the fifteen-year-old J.B. Charbonneau was certainly dwelling apart from the Clark household and was marked off by his race. Years later, he is reported to have met Clark's nephew and son at Fort Laramie; they remembered him as someone seen in St. Louis or known to be a student there, not as a family member.[20] At age eighteen, we find young Charbonneau meeting Prince Paul at the mouth of the Kansas River. He was already living on his own, far from Clark, far from his father. According to Clark's notes on the cover of a cash book and journal for 1825–1828, Toussaint Charbonneau was then among the Mandans, "Se car ja we au" was dead, and their son was in "Wertenburgh," Germany. That family was now dissolved, and Clark could pen this final account of it.[21] Alas, the infant Pomp, Clark's darling, dancing Baptiste, did not become, in fact, his adopted son. "I will educate him and treat him as my own child" — these words turned out to be an exaggeration, or an extravagant promise that could be only half fulfilled.

Still, Clark deserves credit for staying as true to his word as he did. As a young man just parting from the expedition, he could hardly foresee all that he was getting into by asking to take on an infant. The child's parents changed their plans more than once. Clark himself changed his home and his profession, married, and began his own family. The baby grew up to be a young man with a will of his own, but formal schooling could not wholly prepare him for thriving by himself in St. Louis. It is worth noting that in a similar situation, Meriwether Lewis seems to have made promises and then left a young charge bereft. This was Toussaint Jusseaume, the half-Indian son of another interpreter — the one who had proposed rattlesnake powder to ease Sacagawea's labor. Young Jusseaume came to St. Louis in 1809 at age thirteen to become Lewis's apprentice. Shortly afterwards, Lewis left for the East and died.[22]

SO FAR, WE HAVE LOOKED at young Charbonneau as a symbol, but what of the grown man? The child was shaped by others; but the adult, at an early age, must have taken charge of himself. What kind of life did he carve out between 1805 and 1866 and between the courts of Europe and the rough trails of the West? The terms of this question point to extreme contrasts in Charbonneau's career, contrary pulls or tensions on a "half-Indian" in the early nineteenth century. This is a ready formula for further symbolism.

On the one hand, this baby of the expedition may serve as a living clock by which to measure its consequences. The world he first looked out on had uncertain boundaries and horizons in the minds of those around him. His mother remembered her way from the Rockies to the Mandan villages, his French Canadian father might recall the way west from eastern Canada, and soldiers and captains were newly arrived with orders from Thomas Jefferson to explore territory recently held by France and Spain. Through the next sixty years Charbonneau himself would help determine a lasting common map of the West. As an infant, he rode in a party that toiled up a river and bruised their feet on stones and cactus. As an adult guide, he led horse-drawn parties west over two or three separate routes. By the time he died, transcontinental railroads were being financed and built, and eleven states west of the Mississippi had joined the Union. His life spanned the era between Jefferson and the Civil War, through decades of adventure among trappers, soldiers, and prospectors. It is fair to think of Charbonneau as a typical figure of this time, a proper child and survivor of the Lewis and Clark party. To speak precisely, one other member of the expedition, Sgt. Patrick Gass, actually died after Charbonneau did. But Gass — after a long delay — had at last settled down. He married at age sixty, fathered many children, and died in 1870, just short of age ninety-nine. Charbonneau died while still exploring new territories, still prospecting, still on the move, as the last active bachelor–adventurer of the Corps of Discovery. His grave site near Jordan Valley, in this sense, marks the end of the Lewis and Clark Trail.

In another aspect, Charbonneau's life is a symbol not of changing time but of a constant tension in space. He traced a lifelong journey between extremes of East and West. To the east was the attraction or pressure to attain cosmopolitan sophistication — to gain literate education, visit cities and courts, and so rise to a loftier comprehension of the world and its empires. To the west lay raw experience, tests of wits and endurance, daily challenges to survive and press on through unforeseeable risks. If Charbonneau ended his days in the Far West, he also spent many months in Europe, farther east than any other member of the expedition ever traveled. His geographical range stretches much wider than either Lewis's (who learned the way from Monticello to the Pacific) or Jefferson's (who crossed the Atlantic to Paris but never got west of Virginia). His social range also rivals theirs: companion to a prince at court, yet also a valued hand on the western trail. It is tempting to think that he embodied the enduring spirit of Meriwether Lewis — worthy of long conversations with Jefferson, irrepressible in his drive to master the Rockies. But such thoughts rest on sparse and ambiguous records. Jefferson wrote his *Notes on the State of Virginia* and corresponded with dozens of learned men. Lewis recorded pages of extensive, detailed observations useful to science. Charbonneau has left only questionable traces in passages written about him by others.

Just how high were Charbonneau's intellectual attainments? Several western travelers wrote about his talents, and Ann W. Hafen has reprinted three crucial passages. In 1839, a traveler wrote in his diary that a "half-breed" mule driver in his party "had received an education in Europe during seven years." This observer also names him as "a son of Captain Clarke, the great Western traveler and companion of Lewis."[23] The first line may be just as accurate as the second. Another diarist noted more details after meeting Charbonneau at a camp on the Platte River in 1842:

The camp was under the direction of a half-breed, named Chabonard, who proved to be a gentleman of superior information. He had acquired a classic education and could converse quite fluently in German, Spanish, French, and English, as well as several Indian languages. His mind, also, was well stored with choice reading, and enriched by extensive travel and observation. Having visited most of the important places, both in England, France, and Germany, he knew how to turn his experience to good advantage.

There was a quaint humor and shrewdness in his conversation, so garbed with intelligence and perspicuity, that he at once insinuated himself into the good graces of listeners, and commanded their admiration and respect.[24]

These lines seem to describe with precision Charbonneau's superior intelligence, reading, and fluency. On second glance, however, the eye catches that phrase about his "quaint humor and shrewdness." Was Charbonneau playing up to his sudden visitors, boasting, and flourishing just enough remembered German and Spanish to win their respect as an exceptional fur trapper? This encounter lasted just a few hours at most on an island in the Platte where Charbonneau was stuck with a cargo of furs he could not get downstream until the river rose. A third encounter at Bent's Fort in 1844 left another observer with a more cautious or measured idea of Charbonneau's literacy: "I also learned considerable from the hunters of Bent's Fort, particularly from Charbenau, an educated half-breed" who had been the "small Indian papoose" of the Lewis and Clark expedition. "He had been educated to some extent." More important was his skill here and now: "It was said that Charbenau was the best man on foot on the plains or in the Rocky Mountains."[25]

This point deserves some emphasis. High intelligence and skills in several languages do not make a scholar or even much of a sophisticate. Simply to speak with the observers just quoted Charbonneau would have had to know English. As a child he would have heard English, French, Shoshone, and Hidatsa spoken around him for years before he went to school. French was the language of his father and of the schools in St. Louis. In Germany, he would have picked up some German. Anyone may seem remarkable who recalls snatches of many languages, including a few quotations from "choice reading" he may have overheard, but was Charbonneau a practiced reader or writer? There is no evidence of it. There can be little doubt that he could read and handle written documents, for he served as a minor court officer in California for a time and a few surviving court documents have been put forth as samples of his handwriting.[26] Still, nothing more can be said about what he knew of any academic discipline. There are no firm indications that he received advanced training of any kind in Europe or during his long years in the West.

Prince Paul of Württemberg wrote a narrative of his travels in America in 1822–1824, in which he barely mentions meeting Charbonneau and taking him along on his return.[27] Over twenty-five years later, on a trip that took him to California, the duke saw young Indian men, particularly some Shoshones, employed at Sutter's Fort. "One of these Snakes was a fine young lad, quite intelligent," he wrote, "who reminded me strangely and with a certain sadness of B. Charbonneau, who had followed me in 1823 to Europe, and whose mother was of the tribe of the Sho-sho-nis."[28] These few lines seemed to be the best surviving evidence about their years together.[29]

Worse yet, Paul's language was embellished in the 1930s by an enthusiastic translator, Prof. Louis C. Butscher of the University of Wyoming. Butscher was a colleague of Grace Hebard, who enlisted his help while pursuing her studies of Sacagawea. Hebard's book, published in 1933, presents the lines about what Prince Paul saw and wrote in California just as they are quoted here. Hebard also printed a facsimile of Paul's manuscript page and carefully cited her source: "These fragments from the travel diary of Duke Paul

William of Würtemberg were transcribed for the author by Friedrich Bauser of Stuttgart, Germany, archivist, from the Würtemberg state library, roll IX, 521-23 inclusive."[30]

A later translator, working from the original manuscript, uses even fewer words for the passage quoted above: "One of these Snake Indians was a very bright fellow and reminded me of the B. Charboneau who followed me to Europe in 1823 and whose mother was a Schôshô-né."[31] The facsimile supports this brief translation. Butscher, however, enlarged these few words into a full paragraph about Charbonneau. He made some glaring errors and repeated a habit, detected elsewhere in his translations, of adding material that can nowhere be found in his original. (To make matters worse, much of what remained of Prince Paul's original writings and collections was destroyed by Allied bombing in World War II.) In 1965, Ann W. Hafen used part of Butscher's translation in her biographical article about Charbonneau, then added further inferences and speculations. Accounts based on Hafen's work have been distorted ever since. Here, in full, is Butscher's elaborated paragraph:

Among these latter [Shoshones] was a handsome youth who reminded me, on account of his startling likeness, of a lad of the same tribe whom I took to Europe with me from a fur-trading post at the mouth of the Kansas, in western Mississippi in the fall of 1823, and who was my companion there on all my travels over Europe and northern Africa until 1829, when he returned with me to America in 1829. This latter was the son of a Shoshone woman who with her husband, a Canadian Frenchman, accompanied the Messrs. Lewis and Clarke on their expedition to the Pacific Coast in 1804–1806, the one as guide and the other as interpreter. The boy was born on the return trip, and when still quite young, General William Clarke asked the mother's permission to take him to St. Louis in order that he might have him educated at the Catholic Brothers' Seminary.[32]

Hafen quoted selectively from this passage. She ignored Butscher's obvious mistakes that the Kansas River flows in Mississippi and that Sacagawea gave birth on the way back from the Pacific. If she had read further details of Paul's biography, she might have noted that he traveled to Africa in 1839 — a full decade after Charbonneau returned to America. Hafen also ignored the discrepancies between the Butscher paragraph and Hebard's citation and facsimile, though she cited them, too. She focused on the line that Charbonneau was the prince's travel companion in Europe for several years. Out of this hint and further information about the prince, she wove a romance:

For the next six years Baptiste did not see his native land. He lived with Prince Paul in a fine castle about thirty miles from Stuttgart, Germany, in a verdant woodland. There he studied the languages which later made him an excellent interpreter. With Prince Paul he visited the interesting spots of France, England, Germany, and Africa.[33]

Hafen found remarks about the prince's character, that he was "utterly democratic and considerate in all his dealings with others" and once declared himself entrapped in a palace, ever hungering "for the vast silent places and the simple life among free unaffected children of nature." The obvious inference follows: "With tastes such as these, it is not strange that Prince Paul should choose this lad Baptiste for a fellow traveler."[34] Hafen goes on to send Charbonneau on a luxurious grand tour, combining fine horsemanship with book learning, joining him with the prince in brilliant conversations and a passionate interest in science.

THE TROUBLE WITH THIS REASONING is that it turns a solid castle near Stuttgart into a castle in air. Did the duke see to Charbonneau's further education, treat him as an equal, and share his interests? It is just as possible that in Germany he treated the young American as little more than an exotic specimen, a living Indian brought back with other items for his collections. In fact, Grace Hebard raised just this point in her book by reproducing a painting she located in 1930, with the title *Prince Paul, Baptiste, and the Indians*. This image shows the prince in European clothing seated on the ground against a background of enormous tree trunks and a few tepees oddly crammed between them. Dozens of naked or almost naked Indians surround him. Hebard's caption reads: "Prince Paul, in dark clothing, is seated facing Baptiste, the Indian wearing roached hair, and holding a long pipe in his hand." She credits the painting to Balduin Möllhausen and reports that it was discovered by the same Stuttgart archivist who transcribed Paul's journals for her. Hebard does not stress this point, but the painting as she presents it clearly implies a stark inequality: to be recorded with the duke, young Charbonneau was expected to strip, shave his head, sit on the ground, and pose as a man of the wilderness![35]

Much better information about this painting, however, has recently been published by Monika Firla, a Stuttgart researcher with a special interest in exotic figures at the courts of European noblemen. For a study of Duke Paul, Firla advertised in a Stuttgart newspaper and so learned of a privately held lithograph of the scene Hebard had printed. By following other research leads, she also unearthed an important discovery about Charbonneau and some telling information about another exotic young man who came into the duke's court after his second excursion in the Americas.

The painting that Hebard reproduced now hangs in the Deutschordensmuseum in Bad Mergentheim. Firla reviewed its history and examined details in its composition and coloring, and of course she noted its close similarities to the newly discovered lithograph. Her article, amply illustrated, was published in 2000 — but in the specialized journal of a German regional historical society.[36] Only a handful of North American libraries have

This painting was published in 1933 by Grace Hebard as Prince Paul, Baptiste, and the Indians *and credited to Balduin Möllhausen. Recent research indicates that the artist of the gouache is very likely Prince Paul of Württemberg and the title is* Camp of the Kansa Indians on the Blue River, on July 3, 1832. Chiefs Wakan-zie and Sa-ba-No-sche.

holdings of this journal, and thus no student of Lewis and Clark knew of this research until it was mentioned in a permission letter for the use of the painting for this essay.

One of Firla's leading points is that the caption on the lithograph print was probably written by the duke himself. It can be translated as follows:

> Camp of the Kanzas at the Blue River, the 3rd of July 1823.
> Chiefs Wakan-zie and Sa-ba-No-sche.

These ascription lines appear just below the image: "Drawn by Duke Paul of Württemberg" (left) and "Drawn in stone at the royal lithographic office" (right). All this information nicely matches the duke's account of events around July 3, 1823. On July 4, Paul Wilhelm met with Kansa Indians near the mouth of the Blue River, downstream on the Missouri from the mouth of the Kansas River (in present-day Kansas City, Missouri). He seems to have acted as a quasi-official figure in a formal council, for he read out a treaty they showed him and received promises and gifts from chiefs named Wa-kan-ze-re and Sa-ba-no-tsché (in the spelling of his *Travels*). The duke took time to write out several paragraphs about these Indians and their gifts, with particular attention to the near nakedness of the people, their interest in his gun, their knives in leather sheaths, and their gifts of a peace pipe and a special bow and arrows. All these details can be seen in the painting — including the peace pipe, which still survives in the collections of the Canadian Museum of Civilization.[37] From this evidence, Firla reasons that the figure holding the peace pipe in the painting is not Jean Baptiste Charbonneau, as Hebard stated, but Wakanzere.

Perhaps a different figure represents Charbonneau — the fully clothed figure standing directly behind and to the right of the seated Wakanzere. In the lithograph version, this man has young features despite his thick muttonchop whiskers, and his eyes are fixed on the duke. The painting shows the duke and two Indian leaders; that much seems certain. Except for the duke, the figures in European clothes could be interpreters, men from the nearby trading posts, or members of Paul Wilhelm's traveling party. We simply cannot tell. It seems clear that anyone eager to see an authentic image of Jean Baptiste Charbonneau should be cautioned that the odds are against finding it. An intense searcher could well find himself squinting at a moonbeam disguised as a cobweb.

Firla also points out that the duke had met the young Charbonneau in June 1823, just a few days earlier than the meeting with the Kansa Indians at an outpost of Auguste Chouteau's fur-trading company. The duke had come up the Missouri on a company vessel, bearing official backing and direct advice from meetings in St. Louis with Chouteau himself. He remained in the area for about three weeks, lodging with Chouteau's agents. Young Charbonneau was stationed at one of those trading outposts, probably as an apprentice or assistant fur trader. Another recently discovered document, Charbonneau's baptism record of 1809, names this same Auguste Chouteau as the child's godfather and identifies Chouteau's young daughter, Eulalie, as the godmother.[38] Firla does not mention this document, but it could explain how Charbonneau happened to be at the mouth of the Kansas in 1823 and why the duke might have paid particular attention to him. Charbonneau's godfather (along with William Clark) might have helped give him a start in the fur trade and later mentioned him or even commended him to the duke before he set out on his travels.

A more intriguing discovery is that young Charbonneau fathered a child in Germany shortly before he returned to America. At Firla's request, a search was made of the parish birth and death records in Bad Mergentheim. The search produced the name of Anton Fries, who was born on February 20, 1829, and died on May 15 the same year. His parents are named as "Johann Baptist Charbonnau of St. Louis 'called the American' in the service of Duke Paul of this place and Anastasia Katharina Fries, unmarried daughter of the late Georg Fries, a soldier here."[39]

Detail of J.B. Charbonneau's baptismal record, dated December 1809 in St. Louis, in which the space for the mother's name is left blank and the father's name is signed with a mark

To illuminate this brief record, Firla scrupulously examined the remaining documents concerning a similar figure at the duke's court. She reports that Paul Wilhelm followed a common practice of German noblemen and brought back foreign servants from his world travels. In addition to Charbonneau, he brought back a mixed-blood Indian from Mexico, two Africans, and a "small Indian" named Antonio. This arrangement, according to Firla, gave the duke "the advantage of having an informant at command, who could give information out of his own background training, if there was some question about his culture."[40] In short, such persons were on call to serve and instruct the duke; their own advantage was secondary to their usefulness to him.

The Mexican servant, Johann (Juan) Alvarado, may have filled the role of Charbonneau's successor, for he came to Germany in 1831, after Charbonneau had returned to St. Louis. Alvarado's surviving records include a few letters and an inventory of his effects, made at his death in 1841 at the age of twenty-six. Firla uses these items to make an evenhanded estimate of how Alvarado fitted into live in the duke's household. Certainly he was an underling and a dependent. He wore the duke's livery, which reverted to the household stores at his death, and his other effects hardly offset his burial expenses. When the duke traveled to Africa, Alvarado had no choice but to go along — and experience hazards that almost led to his drowning. Like other servants from abroad, he was rebaptized as a Lutheran at the duke's behest. At the same time, Alvarado enjoyed some clear advantages. He owned a few pieces of jewelry, some souvenirs from his travels, and his own silks and satins. He also had a handful of schoolbooks, evidence that the duke had seen to his education in basic geography, history, arithmetic, French, and Spanish. Alvarado's letters show that he could manage a little formal German, stiffly, with the aid of a guidebook on proper letterforms. He was trained in bookbinding and served as a *Kammerdiener*, which most likely means that he supervised some lackeys and table-waiters. On occasion he had a hand in setting off festive fireworks displays for the court.

One record calls Alvarado the duke's *Günstling*, a term that could be derogatory (his minion) or positive (a man enjoying his favor). Firla stresses the positive, noting that Alvarado was lamented when he died, even by one of his creditors. The duke saw to his proper burial and the payment of his debts. Alvarado himself claimed that the duke — a notorious pennypincher — paid him his wages on time and in full and that he earned enough to put aside some savings. Firla emphasizes that Alvarado was accepted as a servant of many talents and was not labeled as a person of a different race. Like Charbonneau, Alvarado had a liaison with a local unmarried woman (a young housemaid) and fathered a child, for which he feared the duke's indignation but not any racist resentment. The Württemberg court seems to have accepted these men as servants, not display items, and Charbonneau's paternity record is notable for calling him simply "the American."

Nonetheless, Firla's emphasis on the positive cannot obscure the fact that both Charbonneau and Alvarado led confined lives in Germany. For all their moderate comforts, they depended on the favor of the duke. They were at his command, afraid of his displeasure, surrounded by his realm, and with little prospect of marriage or independence, whatever their training. It could not be certain that either would ever return to his homeland (in fact, Alvarado died after ten years in the duke's service).

The essential truth, then, is that young Charbonneau traveled to Europe and no doubt had some kind of learning experience in the course of his six years there. But exactly what and how he learned are not known. Unfortunately, the notion has often been repeated that he went off to Europe in order to improve his mind by formal study and traveled widely as the close companion of a prince. Hafen asserts this idea, as we have seen. Irving Anderson repeats it, quoting Hafen.[41] Charles G. Clarke repeats it in his widely used source, *The Men of the Lewis and Clark Expedition*, citing Hafen.[42] Finally, the biographical sketch of Charbonneau in the modern scholarly edition of the Lewis and Clark journals refers readers to Hafen, Clarke, and Anderson.[43]

This interpretive sign at the grave site in the Jordan Valley identifies Charbonneau as "the youngest member of the Lewis and Clark Expedition." "Baptiste and his mother," the text continues, "symbolized the peaceful nature of the 'Corps of Discovery.' "

As a result of this inflated notion, at least two authors are embarrassed by Charbonneau's subsequent life story. How could such a man of refinement spend the rest of his life at hard labor on western trails, far from books and the pleasures of fine intellect? Grace Hebard believed Charbonneau made his way to the Shoshone reservation in Wyoming after 1852 and "reverted in later years to his Indian customs and manner of life." She sees this as a degeneration: "In later life he seems to have deteriorated despite his education [and] his contact with civilization." On this note, she concludes her chapter about him: "Culture that is only a veneering is easily rubbed off by constant association with uneducated Indians and illiterate whites."[44] Hafen sees Charbonneau's later career more romantically, as a yielding to the irresistible call of the wild. Lacking direct evidence, she quotes from an unidentified "educated Indian" who explained in 1839 why he chose to "leave civilized life for a precarious livelihood in the wilderness":

OHS neg., OrHi 103121

One of two known samples of J.B. Charbonneau's handwriting is a one-sentence message in basic Spanish. The other sample consists of brief legal documents in English. Both may be copies made by a clerk and should be viewed with caution.

The Indian's eye cannot be satisfied with the *description* of things, however beautiful soever may be the style, or the harmonies of verse in which it is conveyed. For neither the periods of burning eloquence, nor the mighty and beautiful creations of the imagination, can unbosom the treasures and realities as they live in their own native magnificence on the eternal mountains, and in the secret untrodden vale. . . .

I must range the hills, I must always be able to out-travel my horses, I must always be able to strip my own wardrobe from the backs of the deer and buffalo, and to feed upon their rich loins; I must always be able to punish my enemy with my own hand, or I am no longer an Indian.

Hafen seriously contends that such a romantic aria "could well have come" from Charbonneau's own lips.[45] At root, the implication is the same in both authors: Charbonneau chose wilderness over civilization. He deliberately turned his back on Europe to choose America, set his face west instead east, and for worse or better led the life of an Indian in preference to life in a palace.[46]

More matter-of-fact explanations might have been offered. When the prince returned and parted from Charbonneau (for whatever reasons), the son of Sacagawea had to find his own way. He was then twenty-four years old. There were few opportunities for a penniless courtier along the Mississippi in 1829, fewer still for a German-speaking "half-breed." William Clark and others were involved in the fur trade and could give him a modest start on a plain way of making a living. Furthermore, there could have been a deeply ingrained predilection working within him quite apart from Indian racial longings or the occult spell of the wilderness. All the great models of masculine achievement in his life had put their lives at risk by pushing west: his father, Lewis, Clark, the great traders of St. Louis, and Prince Paul, who had left his young wife and newborn child to return for another adventure in America. It seems pointedly odd that Paul of Württemberg did not take Charbonneau deeper into America on this 1829 return trip. He applied to William Clark for a passport with permission to cross "to the Columbia and Pacific Ocean," and Grace Hebard has found 1830 and 1833 records of Paul dealing with Charbonneau's father; but there are no dealings with the son after 1829.[47] If the prince was close to young Charbonneau, had traveled widely with him, and knew him to be the child of the Lewis and Clark project, then why not enjoy his companionship on this reenactment of scientific exploration across the continent? It could be that the younger man did not reject the East at all but spent years in a vain chase west, pursuing the phantom of the exploring father–patron–commander who had vanished — until he himself became a knowledgeable guide and man of the western trail.

CHARBONNEAU'S CAREER IN THE West raises a different problem of split identity if we consider his relations to western Indians. As a guide, interpreter, prospector, and minor official, he had a hand in displacing or exploiting aboriginal peoples and ways of life. In other words, far from becoming either Hebard's degenerate Indian or Hafen's romantic man of the wild, the records show Charbonneau hard at work supporting white invaders. In the Mormon Battalion, he guided an armed force explicitly recruited to help seize New Mexico and California.[48] As *alcalde,* or magistrate, of the San Luis Rey Mission near San Diego, he imposed harsh sentences on Indian workers. As a placer miner in the gold rush, he was on the scene of crucial forays against local Indians and the exploitation of Indian labor such as Prince Paul witnessed when he visited Sutter's settlement. Often referred to as a "half-breed," Charbonneau knew the commonplace racism of his time; he had to make his way through raw conflicts by complying with it.

In 1848, for example, he resigned as *alcalde* at the San Luis Rey Mission, because whites distrusted him. According to an official report, he said that he had "done his duty to the best of his ability, but being 'a half-breed Indian of the U.S. is regarded by the people as favoring the Indians more than he should do, and hence there is much complaint against him.'"[49] A history of the mission, however, reviews other documents and shows that Charbonneau's sentences could be severe. In one case, he awarded fifty-one dollars to the proprietor of a general store to be paid by an Indian who would serve that proprietor at the rate of twelve and a half cents a day. In effect, it was a sentence to perpetual slavery.[50] The mission historian, Zyphyrin Englehart, charitably suggests that such sentences were so intolerable to Charbonneau that he resigned. Irving Anderson puts it more forcefully: he resigned "because of his concern for human dignity in the treatment of certain Indians as virtual slaves."[51] But his motives are beyond our knowing. The record shows only that he issued such harsh penalties, which Englehart and Anderson display as the only authentic samples of Charbonneau's hand.

After this experience, Charbonneau may well have played down or suppressed his Indian parentage. Hafen quotes another forty-niner whose "heart was gladdened by the appearance of other white men, not hostile, at his camp, in the person of J.B. Charbonneau, Jim Beckwourth, and Sam Mayers, all noted mountaineers."[52] Charbonneau's most extensive obituary was written by someone who had known him in Placer County, California, since 1852. It describes him simply as a California pioneer, mentions that his mother was "a half breed of the Crow tribe," and hastens to report that he spent years in Europe learning languages. Not a word is included about Sacagawea or Lewis and Clark or about the Mormon Battalion or the years at San Luis Rey, though the writer regrets he lacks more information about a colorful life "lived among stirring and eventful scenes." Charbonneau, he concludes, "was of pleasant manners, intelligent, well read in the topics of the day, and was generally esteemed in the community in which he lived, as a good meaning and inoffensive man." The writer evidently longs to be more definite, but his obscure neighbor had stories he never told.[53]

T HIS PRESENT REVIEW OF Charbonneau's life is necessarily critical of earlier research and of current efforts to recast him into a symbol. It must be said that Hebard, Hafen, and Anderson have turned up much valuable evidence after diligent searching, but they presented their discoveries all too blandly, and inconsistently, in accounts of a strangely charmed life. As interest in Lewis and Clark intensifies, we can expect that Sacagawea's baby, now gleaming on the coin, will be celebrated further. His life story will be repeated, these sources will be cited, and their distortions and misunderstandings will be wildly amplified. A reader of history needs some countervailing cautions.

The problem is not that Charbonneau will become or remain a mysterious, symbolic figure. It is rather that he can be nothing else. Like every historical figure worth discussing, he is reshaped by the stories others make about him and that then get firmly attached. Even prolific writers suffer from the same root problem. George Washington is forever the Father of his

Country, Jefferson is the Sage of Monticello, and Franklin is the exemplar of thrift, even though historians continue to sift whole libraries of their works and challenge those simple labels.

Because he leaves no memorable words of his own, Charbonneau is prey to some peculiar fantasizing. As we have seen, he was observed as a symbol throughout his life, from beginning to end: product of a snake remedy at birth, signal of peace on the trail, memento of Clark's affection and promises in his youth, Indian companion displayed in Europe by a prince, mixed-blood mountain man, self-effacing California pioneer. Take away these symbolic Charbonneaus, and what is left? A name, oddly misspelled here and there in obscure travel diaries, and an image on a statue or a coin. There is no reaching the historic man through these flittering fragments. The historic man has turned to dust. The lingering question is what we will choose to remember and symbolize in our turn.

In my view, Charbonneau was not memorably charmed, learned, heroic, or distinguished. He figures in history primarily as Sacagawea's child. Still, his life course traces a fascinating path between Europe and the West and so raises good questions about American values. Jefferson's ideals of human equality have been put to the test over two centuries, in a country he helped make a continental power. Indifference, prejudice, exploitation, and violent disruptions have beset the peoples who saw soldiers coming, bearing Jefferson's flags, medals, and proclamations. Charbonneau was caught up by those same soldiers and pulled along over rough terrain for sixty years. He has a story worth telling, but not to point a neat symbolic moral. His life matters most for the questions it raises: What symbols do we go on making of him, his mother, and Lewis and Clark?

Notes

The editors are grateful to Roy Reynolds for permission to reprint the image on page 14, Jean Baptiste Charbonneau, *from a series that commemorate the Lewis and Clark Bicentennial. For more information, see www.stagestopgallery.com or call 541-586-3078. The collection has received the endorsement of the National Council of the Lewis & Clark Bicentennial, www.lewisandclark2000.org.*

1. Facts and documents are surveyed in three principal sources: Grace Raymond Hebard, *Sacajawea: Guide of the Lewis and Clark Expedition* (Glendale, Calif.: Arthur H. Clark, 1933), 109–48; Ann W. Hafen, "Jean Baptiste Charbonneau," in Leroy R. Hafen, ed., *The Mountain Men and the Fur Trade of the Far West,* 10 vols. (Glendale, Calif.: Arthur H. Clark, 1965–1972), 1:205–24; and Irving R. Anderson, "J.B. Charbonneau, Son of Sacajawea," *Oregon Historical Quarterly* 71 (1970): 246–64. Perhaps the most widely known general account is Irving W. Anderson's pamphlet "A Charbonneau Family Portrait," often reprinted from *America West* 17 (March–April 1980): 4–13, 58–64; Sandra Reinebach, business manager of Fort Clatsop Historical Association, advises that hundreds of copies are sold at Fort Clatsop each year.

2. Gary Moulton, ed., *The Journals of the Lewis & Clark Expedition,* 13 vols. (Lincoln: University of Nebraska Press, 1983–2001), 3:291.

3. The childbirth of Sacagawea is a famous bit of Lewis and Clark lore. At the recent grave site ceremonies, Michelle Broussard of the National Lewis and Clark Bicentennial Council brought a powder of rattlesnake rattle to scatter over the grave.

4. Similar balances of puzzlement, doubt, and assurance are discussed in my book *Acts of Discovery* (Urbana: University of Illinois Press,

1993), esp. chap. 3, pp. 52–69.

5. Michael J. Lewis, "Of Kitsch and Coins," *Commentary* 108 (October 1999): 32–6.

6. Elliott Coues, ed., *History of the Expedition under the Command of Lewis and Clark*, 3 vols. (1893; reprint, New York: Dover, 1965), 1:257. This sentence evidently derives from Clark's line of November 11, 1804, about "two Squars of the Rock Mountain, purchased from the Indians" by Charbonneau. See Moulton, ed., *Journals*, 3:232–3. Biddle's remark that Charbonneau "married her" is a euphemism, for he possessed, shared, and abandoned many Indian women.

7. Vladimir Nabokov, *Lolita* (New York: Fawcett Crest, 1955), 130. To be fair, we should note that Sacagawea had been promised in marriage by her own people before she reached puberty or was abducted. According to Lewis's information, among the Shoshones a girl of thirteen or fourteen was "surrendered to her sovereign lord and husband agreeably to contract" (Moulton, ed., *Journals*, 5:120). Lewis's vocabulary, however, reveals the marriage bargain for what it was, a trade in women by sovereign lords.

8. Moulton, ed., *Journals*, 5:305.

9. Ibid., 5:305–6.

10. Ibid., 5:267–8.

11. Gerald S. Snyder, *In the Footsteps of Lewis and Clark* (Washington, D.C.: National Geographic Society, 1970); James P. Ronda, *Lewis and Clark among the Indians* (Lincoln: University of Nebraska Press, 1984). The painting is at the Amon Carter Museum in Fort Worth, Texas.

12. Ronda, *Lewis and Clark*, 254.

13. Moulton, ed., *Journals*, 4:10, 29, 157.

14. Ibid., 8:225, 228n.

15. Ibid., 8:305–6.

16. Donald Jackson, ed., *Letters of the Lewis and Clark Expedition with Related Documents*, 2d ed., 2 vols. (Urbana: University of Illinois Press, 1978), 1:315–16.

17. Clark's name appears nowhere on that record, but of course he was not Catholic. The father is named as "Toussaint Charboneau," but he signed with an *X*. The mother is described as "——— Sauvagesse de la nation des Serpents." Bob Moore, "Pompey's Baptism," *We Proceeded On* 26 (February 2000): 10–17.

18. Hebard, *Sacajawea*, 89–90, 114–15.

19. Hebard, *Sacajawea*, 112. The court document leaves many questions unanswered. We cannot know whether the two children named in it were both fathered by Charbonneau; whether either was born to Sacagawea; whether the child named "Toussaint" is actually Jean Baptiste or possibly a younger brother; and whether Clark's name was written into it (in an alteration of the document) at his urging or another's.

20. Hebard, *Sacajawea*, 114–16, 139–40.

21. Jackson, ed., *Letters*, 2:638.

22. Moulton, ed., *Journals*, 3:205n; Stephen E. Ambrose, *Undaunted Courage: Meriwether Lewis, Thomas Jefferson, and the Opening of the American West* (New York: Simon & Schuster, 1996), 438.

23. Hafen, "Jean Baptiste Charbonneau," 214.

24. Ibid., 216, citing Rufus B. Sage, *Rufus B. Sage: His Letters and Papers, 1836–1847*, ed. L.R. and A.W. Hafen, 2 vols. (Glendale, Calif.: Arthur H. Clark, 1956), 2:52–4.

25. Hafen, "Jean Baptiste Charbonneau," 217, citing L.R. Hafen, ed., "The W.M. Boggs Manuscript about Bent's Fort," *Colorado Magazine* 7 (1930): 66–7. Much of this passage is reprinted in facsimile in Hebard, *Sacajawea*, 141, where the spelling and punctuation are somewhat different.

26. Anderson, "J.B. Charbonneau," 260–1, including a facsimile illustration. These handwriting samples should be regarded with caution. As formal documents, they could be copies made by a clerk. They also present a logical enigma. If these are the *only* samples of Charbonneau's hand, how could they be authenticated? What other samples could serve for comparison? The sample of Charbonneau's signature reproduced in *Oregon Historical Quarterly* 72 (1971): 78–9, is subject to the same questions. If the note on which the signature appears is actually in Charbonneau's hand, it reveals that his Spanish was poor at best.

27. The pertinent passages are almost identical in two modern translations: Paul Wilhelm, duke of Württemberg, *Travels in North America 1822–1824*, trans. W. Robert Nitske, ed. Savoie Lottinville (Norman: University of Oklahoma Press, 1973), 271, 399; and idem, "First Journey to North America in the Years 1822 to 1824," trans. William G. Bek, *South Dakota Historical Collections* 19 (1938): 303, 444. Lottinville remarks in his introduction to the Nitske translation that Paul had little talent for fascinating human portraits (p. xx), and what Paul says about J.B. Charbonneau is not only brief but also inaccurate — Paul says Charbonneau was sixteen years old in 1823 — and baffling about time sequences: "Baptiste . . . joined me on my return, followed me to Europe, and has since then been with me" (p. 271); months later: "On the ninth the boat reached the Kansas. I remained several hours and picked up the son of Toussaint Charbonneau, who would accompany me to Europe" (p. 300).

28. Hebard, *Sacajawea*, 124n. Hebard and others refer to Paul of Württemberg as a "prince." Technically, his title was *Herzog*, or "duke," rather than *Fürst* or *Prinz*.

29. Offers of documents in return for cash have been made to earlier researchers. See Lottinville's introduction to the Nitske translation of Paul's *Travels*, xxvii. Some of Paul's collections survive and are described and illustrated in Axel Schultze-Thulin, ed., *Indianer der Prärien und Plains* (Stuttgart: Staatliches Museum für Völkerkunde, 1976).

30. Hebard, *Sacajawea*, 124; facsimile, 119.

31. Charles Upson Clark, trans., "Extracts from

the Journals of Prince Paul of Wurtemberg, Year 1850," *Southwestern Journal of Anthropology* 15 (1959): 252; quoted in John A. Hussey, ed., *Early Sacramento: Glimpses of John Augustus Sutter, the Hok Farm and Neighboring Indian Tribes from the Journals of Prince Paul . . . of Württemberg* (Sacramento, Calif.: Sacramento Book Collectors Club, 1973), 59–60. Hussey provides a careful scholarly introduction to Butscher's translation of Paul's journal from his 1850 journey to California, with an especially valuable account of Butscher as translator (pp. 22–5).

32. Hussey, ed., *Early Sacramento*, 59.

33. Hafen, "Jean Baptiste Charbonneau," 210.

34. Ibid., 210–11. Here, too, Hafen leans on Butscher, quoting from his biographical essay on the duke. See Louis C. Butscher, "A Brief Biography of Prince Paul Wilhelm of Württemberg (1797–1860), *New Mexico Historical Review* 17 (1942): 180–225. In context, the remark that he was "utterly democratic" was written by Balduin Möllhausen, who was not born until 1825 and here describes the prince as he knew him in 1851 (p. 217); the remark about being trapped in a palace is part of a fictitious anecdote (p. 190).

35. Hebard, *Sacajawea*, 12. Möllhausen traveled to America with Paul on later expeditions, and it seems unlikely he saw Charbonneau. This painting is reproduced in Nitske's translation of Paul's *Travels* after page 254, where it is captioned "Sioux Camp, watercolor, probably by Rosshirt from suggestions by Duke Paul of Württemberg (Courtesy Stadt Bad Mergentheim)." Neither source provides fuller information. See also Hebard, *Sacajawea*, 134, for reference to an oil painting seen in Stuttgart in 1927 titled "Prince Paul and His Indian Boy." It should be noted that Paul was only eight years older than J.B. Charbonneau.

36. Monika Firla, "Die anonyme Gouache 'Herzog Paul von Württemberg bei den Indianern' und die neuentdeckte Lithographie 'Lager der Kanzas am blauen Fluss, den 3ten July 1823. Häuptlinge Wakan-zie und Sa-ba-No-sche' nach einer Zeich-nung des Herzogs," *Württembergisch Franken: Jahrbuch des Historischen Vereins für Württem-bergish Franken* 84 (2000): 259–87.

37. Firla, "Die anonyme Gouache," 269–73, reprints pages from the *Travels* (see the Nitske translation, 280–5).

38. Bob Moore, "Pompey's Baptism," *We Proceeded On* 26:1 (February 2000): 10–17, esp. 15.

39. Monika Firla, "Johann Alvarado (1815–41), Ein mexicanischer Kammerdiener Herzog Paul Wilhelms von Württemberg in Mergentheim," *Württembergisch Franken: Jahrbuch des Historischen Vereins für Württembergish Franken*

83 (1999): 247–60, 248n3 (my translation).

40. Firla, "Alvarado," 249 (my translation).

41. Anderson, "J.B. Charbonneau," 249.

42. Charles G. Clarke, *The Men of the Lewis and Clark Expedition* (Glendale, Calif.: Arthur H. Clark, 1970): 148–9.

43. Moulton, ed., *Journals*, 3:291n.

44. Hebard, *Sacajawea*, 147–8.

45. Hafen, "Jean Baptiste Charbonneau," 213–14.

46. The notion that Charbonneau chose wilderness was circulated in his own lifetime. Mountain man James Beckwourth dictated a memoir published in 1856 that included a confused passage about the Humboldt River. He stated that it was named St. Mary's River in honor of Mary, the wife of Chapineau, who was guide and interpreter to Lewis and Clark. Mary gave birth to a child on the banks of this river. William Clark "adopted the child thus rudely issued into the world, and on his return to St. Louis took the infant with him, and baptized it John Baptist Clark Chapineau. After a careful culture of his mind, the boy was sent to Europe to complete his education. But the Indian was ineffaceable in him. The Indian lodge and his native mountain fastnesses possessed greater charms than the luxuries of civilized life. He returned to the desert and passed his days with his tribe." Delmont R. Oswald, ed., *The Life and Adventures of James P. Beckwourth*, as told to Thomas D. Bonner (Lincoln: University of Nebraska Press, 1972), 528. This third-hand conflation of John the Baptist in the desert, St. Mary and a miraculous child, and Clark's attentions to Charbonneau may, just may, contain a glimmer of Charbonneau's own boasting to a friend on the trail.

47. Hebard, *Sacajawea*, 19, 100–4.

48. Norma Baldwin Ricketts, *The Mormon Battalion: U.S. Army of the West, 1846–1848* (Logan: Utah State University Press, 1996), traces the day-by-day progress of this military expedition, summarizing original documents. Ricketts's account of Charbonneau's full career, however, repeats many errors reviewed here (pp. 325–6).

49. J.D. Stevenson to Gov. Mason, July 24, 1848, quoted in Hafen, "Jean Baptiste Charbonneau," 220.

50. Zyphyrin Englehart, *San Luis Rey Mission* (San Francisco: J.H. Berry, 1921), 152; quoted in Anderson, "J.B. Charbonneau," 260–1.

51. Anderson, "A Charbonneau Family Portrait," 63.

52. Hafen, "Jean Baptiste Charbonneau," 221.

53. "Death of a California Pioneer," *Auburn (California) Placer Herald*, July 7, 1866, quoted in Hafen, "Jean Baptiste Charbonneau," 222–3.

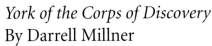